CHORALES AND RHYTHM ETUDES FOR SUPERIOR BANDS

How to Use This Book

Chorales and Rhythm Etudes for Superior Bands is designed to develop skills of musicianship. It focuses on *tone production, balance, blend,* and *technical precision.* The book may be used in a variety of settings. It can be effective for small or large ensembles, in group work, or in private instruction. The text follows the same 16-week instruction calendar found in *Superior Bands in Sixteen Weeks.* The two volumes are complementary; using them together will fortify your skills and understanding.

Many of the exercises in this book will cover the expanse of your instrument range. Octave choices are included for developing players. Using the octave that best suits the needs of each student ensures systematic range development without tone quality compromise. Add range as tone quality improves.

Several percussion instruments are integrated into the exercises. Percussion technique is as critical to ensemble sound development as wind technique. The director should focus on correct percussion performance techniques. Encourage percussionists to be confident in pitched percussion. Bells and other treble clef mallet instruments may play the C instrument line or the top line of the conductor's score.

Good Musicians Always Play With Good
- TONE
- INTONATION
- & TECHNIQUE

Good luck!

THE F·J·H MUSIC COMPANY INC.
Frank J. Hackinson

Production: Frank and Gail Hackinson
Production Coordinator: Philip Groeber
Editors: Deborah A. Sheldon, Brian Balmages, Timothy Loest, and Linda Gammon
Cover: Terpstra Design, San Francisco
Text Design and Layout: K. B. Dalzell
Engraving: Tempo Music Press, Inc.
Printer: Tempo Music Press, Inc.

ISBN-13: 978-1-56939-834-0

Table of Contents

PRACTICE! PRACTICE! PRACTICE!

Two Keys to Becoming a Successful Musician

Proper Playing Position

- Sit on the **edge** of the chair

- Keep feet **flat** on the floor

- **Quietly listen** for instructions

Good Breathing Habits

- **Breathe deeply** and with the diaphragm

- Release the air **slowly with control**

PRACTICE! PRACTICE! PRACTICE!

BAND BALANCE

Balance in the ensemble can be attributed to listening, good tone production, accurate intonation, and blend. The Balance Pyramid will help you understand the role of your instrument in the ensemble sound. Study the chart and these suggestions.

- Listen to yourself. Your sound should blend with the full ensemble. If it does not, make adjustments to blend.

- Listen to your section. The section sound should blend with the full ensemble. If it does not, make adjustments to blend.

- After making necessary adjustments, listen again. If you still don't hear a good blend, tone quality may be a concern. Make necessary adjustments (air stream and breath support, posture, embouchure, reed, tuning slide, mouthpiece, barrel).

- After making those adjustments, listen again. If you still don't hear a good blend, intonation may be a concern. Make necessary adjustments (air stream and breath support, posture, embouchure, reed, tuning slide, mouthpiece, barrel).

Use the following chart or Balance Pyramid* to adjust your sound and balance within the band.

Drums = capstone

Piccolo
Flute
p Oboe
← 4th group

Clarinet
Alto Saxophone
Trumpet
mp Percussion
← 3rd group

Alto Clarinet, Tenor Saxophone
Horn, Trombone
mf
← 2nd group

Bassoon, Bass Clarinet,
Contra Alto and Contra Bass Clarinet,
Baritone Saxophone, Baritone/Euphonium, Tuba
f
← 1st group

Notes to the Director

1. Start by using a tuning note (concert B♭, concert F).

2. Select other notes to train students through the range of the instrument.

3. Always start by using the first group (refer to pyramid), followed by the second, then the third, and finally the fourth. Conduct so that subsequent groups know to listen and play to blend rather than play louder than the previous group.

4. Use compare and contrast techniques to reinforce the sound of good balance. Allow the group to perform with incorrect balance and instruct them to listen. Discuss the qualities of that sound and follow up with a performance using appropriate blend.

**Taken from "Effective Performance of Band Music" by W. Francis McBeth, published by Southern Music.*

CHORALES

The chorales are designed to aid the ensemble in *tone production, balance, blend,* and *intonation*. Listening is a key component in the development of skills in these areas. Connecting the ear and voice are also useful. Directors may teach the singing of the chorales as a prelude to performance on the instruments. Singing will amplify issues of balance and blend, in particular. Breath support necessary for good tone production and intonation with the voice is made clear and is readily transferable to instrumental technique. Some articulations are indicated and others implied. Where no articulation exists, assume legato tonguing.

Chorale Index

No.	Time Signature	Key Center
1.	$\frac{4}{4}$	B♭ Major
2.	$\frac{4}{4}$	G minor
3.	$\frac{4}{4}$	E♭ Major
4.	$\frac{4}{4}$	C minor
5.	$\frac{3}{4}$	F Major
6.	$\frac{3}{4}$	D minor
7.	$\frac{2}{4}$	A♭ Major
8.	$\frac{6}{8}$	F minor
9.	$\frac{3}{4}$	D♭ Major
10.	$\frac{4}{4}$	B♭ minor
11.	$\frac{4}{4}$	C Major
12.	$\frac{4}{4}$	A minor
13.	$\frac{4}{4}$	G Major
14.	$\frac{4}{4}$	E minor
15.	$\frac{6}{8}$	D Major
16.	$\frac{3}{4}$	B minor

Chorale No. 1
(B♭ Major)

Conductor's Score

Bells play top line of Conductor's Score

C Instruments (Flutes divisi - Oboe plays the bottom line)

B♭ Instruments

*B♭ Bass Clarinet (if only one player, play the bottom line)

*Contra Bass Clarinet plays the bottom line throughout.

Chorale No. 1
(B♭ Major)

Baritone T.C. and B♭ Tenor Saxophone (if only one player, play the bottom line - Tenor Sax plays the top line)

E♭ Instruments

E♭ Baritone Saxophone

E♭ Alto and Contra Alto Clarinets

F Instruments (if only one player, play the bottom line)

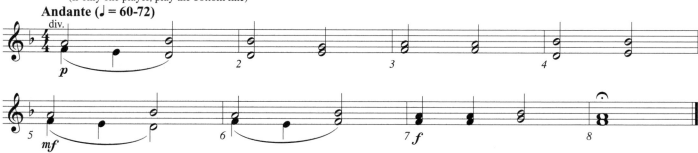

Bass Clef Instruments (Trombone 1 plays the top line - Trombone 2 and Baritone play the middle line - Tuba plays the bottom line)

BB206

Chorale No. 2
(G minor)

Chorale No. 2
(G minor)

Baritone T.C. and B♭ Tenor Saxophone (if only one player, play the bottom line - Tenor Sax plays the top line)

E♭ Instruments

E♭ Baritone Saxophone

E♭ Alto and Contra Alto Clarinets

F Instruments (if only one player, play the bottom line)

Bass Clef Instruments (Trombone 1 plays the top line - Trombone 2 and Baritone play the middle line - Tuba plays the bottom line)

Chorale No. 3

(E♭ Major)

Conductor's Score

Chorale No. 3
(E♭ Major)

Baritone T.C. and B♭ Tenor Saxophone (if only one player, play the bottom line - Tenor Sax plays the top line)

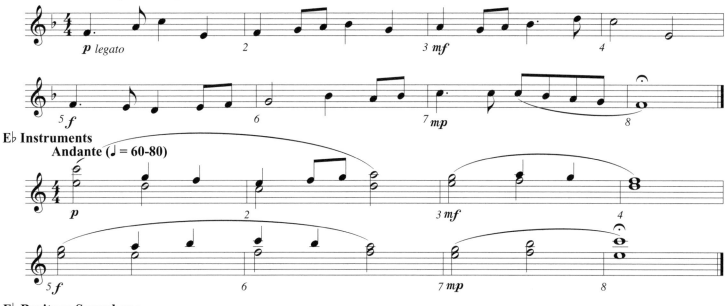

E♭ Instruments

E♭ Baritone Saxophone

E♭ Alto and Contra Alto Clarinets

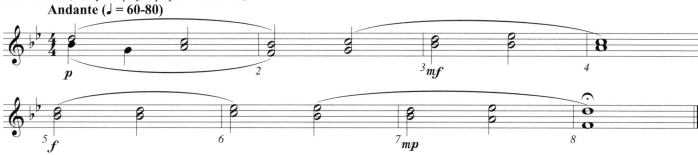

F Instruments (if only one player, play the bottom line)

Bass Clef Instruments (Trombones and Baritone play the top line - Tuba plays the bottom line)

Chorale No. 4
(C minor)

Chorale No. 4
(C minor)

Baritone T.C. and B♭ Tenor Saxophone (if only one player, play the bottom line - Tenor Sax plays the top line)

Espressivo (♩ = 68-72)

E♭ Instruments (if only one player, play the bottom line)

E♭ Baritone Saxophone

E♭ Alto and Contra Alto Clarinets

F Instruments (if only one player, play the bottom line)

Bass Clef Instruments (Trombone 1 plays the top line - Trombone 2 and Baritone play the middle line - Tuba plays the bottom line)
(if only one Trombone or Baritone, play the middle line)

Espressivo (♩ = 68-72)

Chorale No. 5

(F Major)

Chorale No. 5
(F Major)

Baritone T.C. and B♭ Tenor Saxophone (if only one player, play the bottom line - Tenor Sax plays the top line)

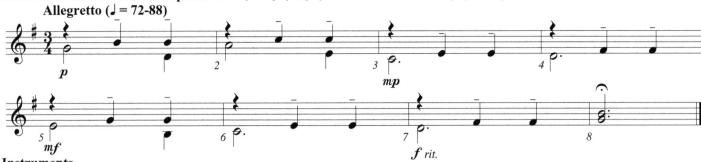

E♭ Instruments

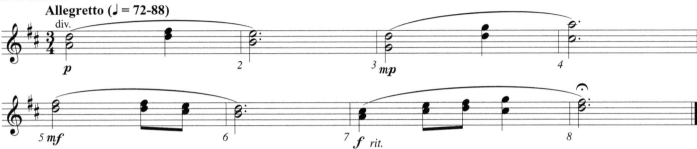

E♭ Baritone Saxophone

E♭ Alto and Contra Alto Clarinets

F Instruments (if only one player, play the bottom line)

Bass Clef Instruments (Trombone 1 plays the top line - Trombone 2 and Baritone play the middle line - Tuba plays the bottom line)

Allegretto (♩ = 72-88) (if only one Trombone or Baritone, play the middle line)

BB206

Chorale No. 6
(D minor)

Chorale No. 6
(D minor)

Baritone T.C. and B♭ Tenor Saxophone (if only one player, play the bottom line - Tenor Sax plays the top line)

E♭ Instruments

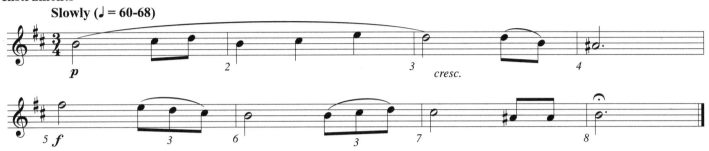

E♭ Baritone Saxophone

E♭ Alto and Contra Alto Clarinets

F Instruments (if only one player, play the bottom line)

Bass Clef Instruments (Trombone 1 plays the top line - Trombone 2 and Baritone play the middle line - Tuba plays the bottom line)
(if only one Trombone or Baritone, play the middle line)

Chorale No. 7

(A♭ Major)

Conductor's Score

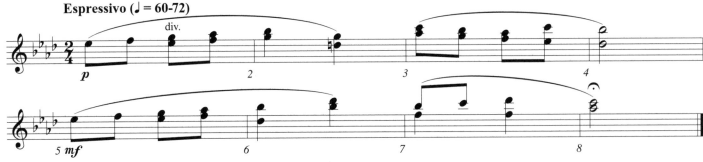

C Instruments (Flutes Divisi - Oboe plays the bottom line)

B♭ Instruments

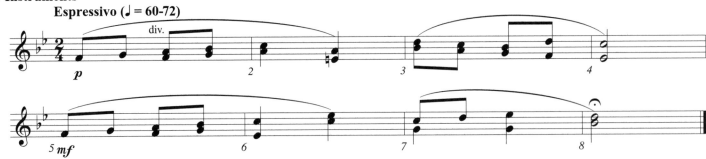

B♭ Bass Clarinet (if only one player, play the bottom line)

Chorale No. 7

(A♭ Major)

Baritone T.C. and B♭ Tenor Saxophone (if only one player, play the bottom line - Tenor Sax plays the top line)

E♭ Instruments

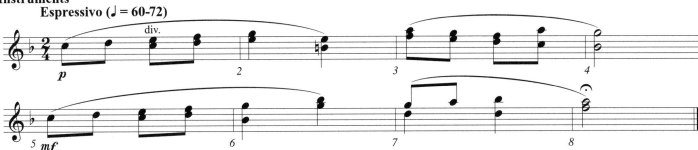

E♭ Baritone Saxophone

E♭ Alto and Contrabass Clarinets

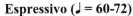

F Instruments (if only one player, play the bottom line)

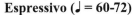

Bass Clef Instruments (Trombone 1 plays the top line - Trombone 2 and Baritone play the middle line - Tuba plays the bottom line)

Espressivo (♩ = 60-72)   (if only one Trombone or Baritone, play the middle line)

BB206

Chorale No. 8

(F minor)

Chorale No. 8
(F minor)

Baritone T.C. and B♭ Tenor Saxophone
Moderato (♩. = 60-80)

E♭ Instruments
Moderato (♩. = 60-80)

E♭ Baritone Saxophone
Moderato (♩. = 60-80)

E♭ Alto and Contra Alto Clarinets
Moderato (♩. = 60-80)

F Instruments (if only one player, play the bottom line)
Moderato (♩. = 60-80)

Bass Clef Instruments (Trombone 1 plays the top line - Trombone 2 and Baritone play the middle line - Tuba plays the bottom line)
Moderato (♩. = 60-80)   (if only one Trombone or Baritone, play the middle line)

Chorale No. 9

(D♭ Major)

Conductor's Score

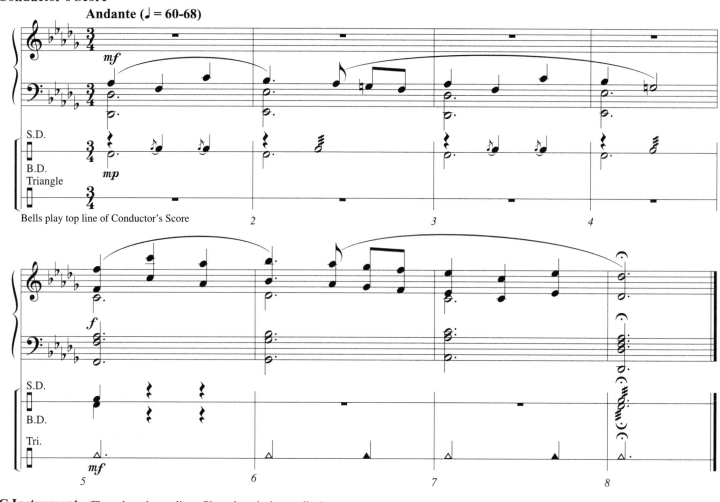

Bells play top line of Conductor's Score

C Instruments (Flute plays the top line - Oboe plays the bottom line)

B♭ Instruments

B♭ Bass Clarinet (if only one player, play the bottom line)

Chorale No. 9
(D♭ Major)

Chorale No. 10
(B♭ minor)

Chorale No. 10
(B♭ minor)

Baritone T.C. and B♭ Tenor Saxophone (if only one player, play the bottom line - Tenor Sax plays the top line)

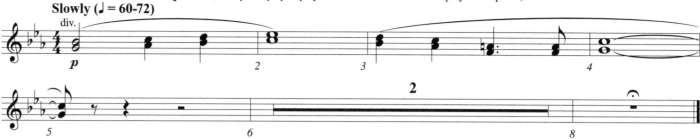

E♭ Instruments

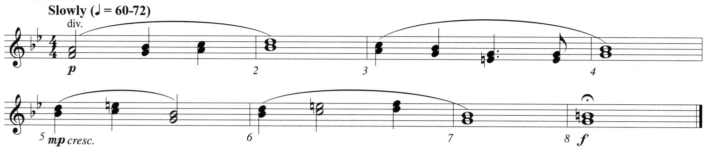

E♭ Baritone Saxophone

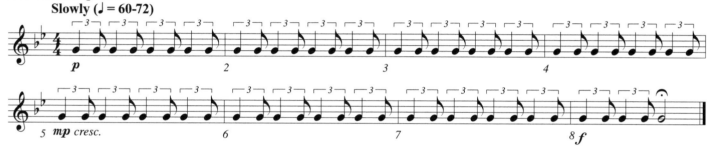

E♭ Alto and Contra Alto Clarinets

F Instruments (if only one player, play the bottom line)

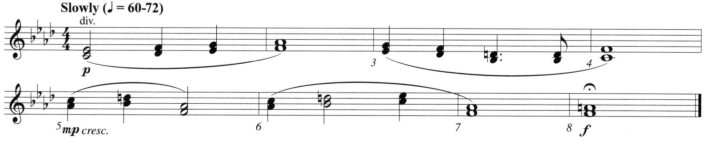

Bass Clef Instruments (Trombone 1 plays the top line - Trombone 2 and Baritone play the middle line - Tuba plays the bottom line)

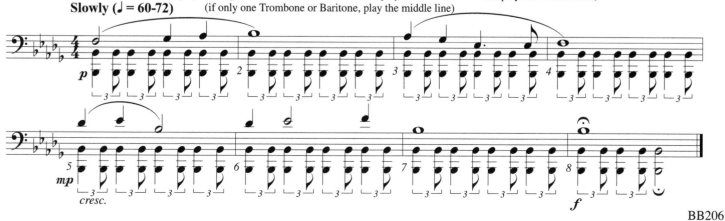

Chorale No. 11
(C Major)

Chorale No. 11
(C Major)

Baritone T.C. and B♭ Tenor Saxophone

E♭ Instruments

E♭ Baritone Saxophone

E♭ Alto and Contra Alto Clarinets

F Instruments (if only one player, play the bottom line)

Bass Clef Instruments (Trombone and Baritone play the top line - Tuba plays the bottom line)

Chorale No. 12
(A minor)

Chorale No. 12
(A minor)

Baritone T.C. and B♭ Tenor Saxophone (if only one player, play the bottom line - Tenor Sax plays the top line)
Andante espressivo (♩ = 60-72)

E♭ Instruments
Andante espressivo (♩ = 60-72)

E♭ Baritone Saxophone
Andante espressivo (♩ = 60-72)

E♭ Alto and Contra Alto Clarinets
Andante espressivo (♩ = 60-72)

F Instruments
Andante espressivo (♩ = 60-72)

Bass Clef Instruments (Trombone 1 plays the top line - Trombone 2 and Baritone play the middle line - Tuba plays the bottom line)
Andante espressivo (♩ = 60-72) (if only one Trombone or Baritone, play the middle line)

Chorale No. 13

(G Major)

Chorale No. 13
(G Major)

Baritone T.C. and B♭ Tenor Saxophone

E♭ Instruments

E♭ Baritone Saxophone

E♭ Alto and Contra Alto Clarinets

F Instruments

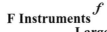

Bass Clef Instruments (Trombone and Baritone play the top line - Tuba plays the bottom line)

Chorale No. 14

(E minor)

Chorale No. 14
(E minor)

Baritone T.C. and B♭ Tenor Saxophone

E♭ Instruments

E♭ Baritone Saxophone

E♭ Alto and Contra Alto Clarinets

F Instruments

Bass Clef Instruments (Trombone 1 plays the top line - Trombone 2 and Baritone play the middle line - Tuba plays the bottom line)

Slowly (♩ = 68-72)   (if only one Trombone or Baritone, play the middle line)

Chorale No. 15
(D Major)

Conductor's Score

Bells play top line of Conductor's Score

C Instruments (Flute plays the top line - Oboe plays the bottom line)

B♭ Instruments

B♭ Bass Clarinet (if only one player, play the bottom line)

Chorale No. 15
(D Major)

Baritone T.C. and B♭ Tenor Saxophone (if only one player, play the bottom line - Tenor Sax plays the top line)

E♭ Instruments

E♭ Baritone Saxophone

E♭ Alto and Contra Alto Clarinets

F Instruments (if only one player, play the bottom line)

Bass Clef Instruments (Trombone 1 plays the top line - Trombone 2 and Baritone play the middle line - Tuba plays the bottom line)

Chorale No. 16
(B minor)

Conductor's Score

Bells play top line of Conductor's Score

C Instruments (Flute plays the top line - Oboe plays the bottom line)

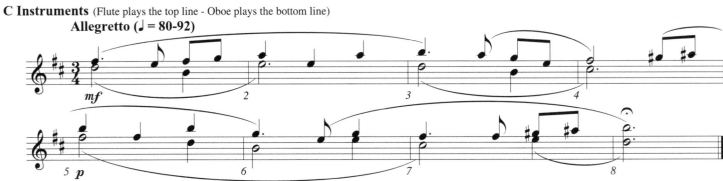

B♭ Instruments

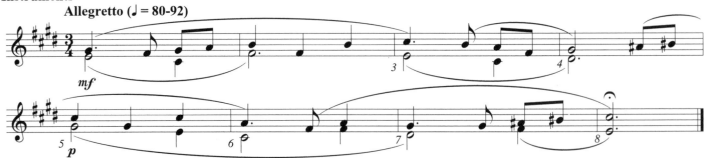

B♭ Bass Clarinet

Chorale No. 16
(B minor)

Baritone T.C. and B♭ Tenor Saxophone
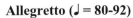

E♭ Instruments

E♭ Baritone Saxophone
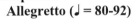

E♭ Alto and Contra Alto Clarinets
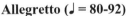
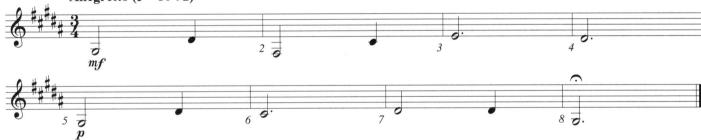

F Instruments (if only one player, play the bottom line)
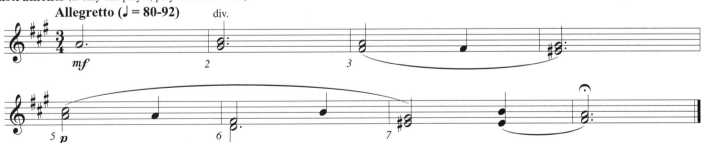

Bass Clef Instruments (Trombone 1 plays the top line - Trombone 2 and Baritone play the middle line - Tuba plays the bottom line)
(if only one Trombone or Baritone, play the middle line)
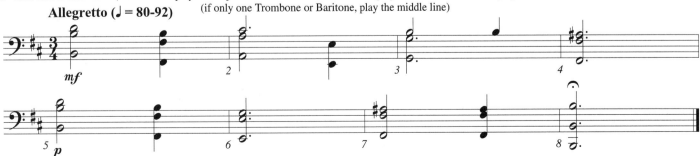

RHYTHM ETUDES

The rhythm etudes are designed to aid the ensemble in *playing, counting,* and *articulating together.* Close attention should be given to *dynamics* and *articulations.* These etudes can be played at various tempi. Notice that the progression of keys used in the rhythm etudes matches that of the chorales to reinforce the weekly sequence of instruction.

Rhythm Instruction Sequence

A. Count each etude aloud

B. Clap each etude

C. Articulate, breathe, and finger each etude with instrument in proper playing position

D. Finally, play the etude

Articulation Hints

STUDENTS MUST MEMORIZE

Normal
Winds use the syllable *Tah* or *Tee*

Legato (long)
Winds use the syllable *Too* or *Doo*

Staccato (short, dry)
Winds use the syllable *Di(t)* or *T*

Accent (normal with emphasis)
Winds use the syllable *Tah* with more emphasis

Rhythm Etude Index

No.	Time Signature	Key Center or Scale	Rhythms and/or Patterns
1.	$\frac{4}{4}$, C	B♭ Major	o, 𝅗𝅥., 𝅗𝅥, 𝅘𝅥, 𝅘𝅥. 𝅘𝅥𝅮
2.	$\frac{3}{4}$	G minor	o, 𝅗𝅥., 𝅗𝅥, 𝅘𝅥, ♫, 𝅘𝅥. 𝅘𝅥𝅮
3.	$\frac{2}{4}$	E♭ Major	𝅘𝅥𝅮𝅘𝅥𝅮𝅘𝅥𝅮, 𝅘𝅥𝅘𝅥, 𝅘𝅥. 𝅘𝅥𝅮
4.	$\frac{4}{4}$	C minor	𝅘𝅥𝅮𝅘𝅥𝅮𝅘𝅥𝅮, 𝅘𝅥𝅘𝅥, 𝅘𝅥. 𝅘𝅥𝅮
5.	$\frac{2}{2}$, ¢	F Major	o, 𝅗𝅥, 𝅘𝅥, 𝅘𝅥. 𝅘𝅥𝅮
6.	$\frac{5}{4}$	D minor	𝅗𝅥, 𝅘𝅥, ♫, 𝅘𝅥𝅮𝅘𝅥
7.	$\frac{4}{4}$	A♭ Major	𝅘𝅥, ♫, 𝅘𝅥𝅮𝅘𝅥, 𝅘𝅥𝅮𝅘𝅥𝅮
8.	$\frac{3}{4}$	F minor	𝅘𝅥, ♫, 𝅘𝅥𝅮𝅘𝅥𝅮𝅘𝅥𝅮, 𝅘𝅥𝅮𝅘𝅥𝅮𝅘𝅥𝅮
9.	$\frac{2}{4}$	D♭ Major	𝅗𝅥, 𝅘𝅥, ♫, 𝅘𝅥𝅮𝅘𝅥𝅮𝅘𝅥𝅮𝅘𝅥𝅮
10.	$\frac{4}{4}$	B♭ minor	♫, 𝅘𝅥𝅮𝅘𝅥𝅮𝅘𝅥𝅮, 𝅘𝅥𝅮𝅘𝅥𝅮𝅘𝅥𝅮𝅘𝅥𝅮, 𝅘𝅥𝅮𝅘𝅥, 𝅘𝅥𝅘𝅥𝅮
11.	$\frac{2}{4}$	C Major	𝅘𝅥𝅮𝅘𝅥𝅮𝅘𝅥𝅮𝅘𝅥𝅮, 𝅘𝅥𝅮𝅘𝅥𝅮𝅘𝅥𝅮, 𝅘𝅥𝅮𝅘𝅥, 𝅘𝅥𝅮𝅘𝅥, 𝅘𝅥𝅘𝅥𝅮, 𝅘𝅥𝅮𝅘𝅥
12.	$\frac{6}{8}$	A minor	𝅘𝅥𝅮𝅘𝅥𝅮𝅘𝅥𝅘𝅥𝅮
13.	$\frac{6}{8}$	G Major	𝅗𝅥., 𝅘𝅥, 𝅘𝅥𝅮𝅘𝅥𝅮, 𝅘𝅥𝅮𝅘𝅥𝅮𝅘𝅥𝅮
14.	$\frac{9}{8}$	E minor	𝅗𝅥., 𝅘𝅥, 𝅘𝅥𝅮𝅘𝅥𝅮, 𝅘𝅥𝅮𝅘𝅥𝅮𝅘𝅥𝅮
15.	$\frac{2}{4}$, $\frac{3}{4}$, $\frac{4}{4}$	D Major	𝅘𝅥, ♫, 𝅘𝅥𝅮𝅘𝅥𝅮, $\overline{}^3\overline{}$
16.	$\frac{6}{8}$, $\frac{2}{4}$, $\frac{4}{4}$	B minor	𝅗𝅥, 𝅘𝅥, ♫, 𝅘𝅥., 𝅘𝅥𝅮𝅘𝅥, 𝅘𝅥𝅮𝅘𝅥𝅮𝅘𝅥𝅘𝅥𝅮

Rhythm Etude No. 1
(B♭ Major)

Rhythm Etude No. 1

(B♭ Major)

C Instruments

Rhythm Etude No. 1
(B♭ Major)

F Instruments

Bass Clef Instruments

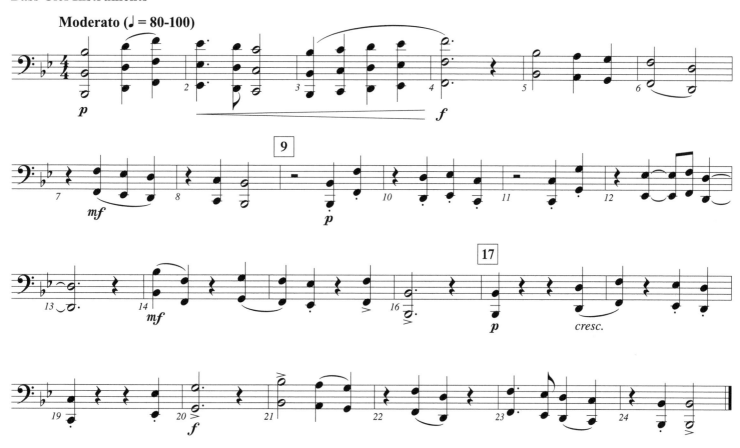

BB206

Rhythm Etude No. 2
(G minor)

Rhythm Etude No. 2

(G minor)

C Instruments

Bb Instruments

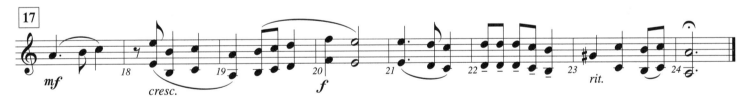

Eb Instruments

Rhythm Etude No. 2
(G minor)

F Instruments

Bass Clef Instruments

Rhythm Etude No. 3
(E♭ Major – Pentatonic)

Rhythm Etude No. 3

(Eb Major – Pentatonic)

C Instruments

Lively folksong (♩ = 112-120)

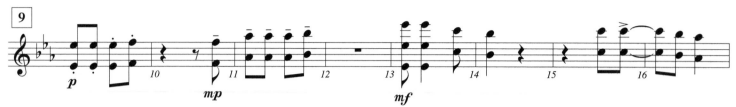

Bb Instruments

Lively folksong (♩ = 112-120)

Eb Instruments

Lively folksong (♩ = 112-120)

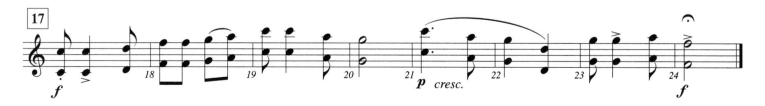

BB206

Rhythm Etude No. 3

(E♭ Major – Pentatonic)

F Instruments

Bass Clef Instruments

Rhythm Etude No. 4
(C minor – Blues/Rock)

Rhythm Etude No. 4
(C minor – Blues/Rock)

50

Rhythm Etude No. 4

(C minor – Blues/Rock)

F Instruments

Bass Clef Instruments

Rhythm Etude No. 5

(F Major)

Conductor's Score

Alla marcia (♩ = 120-132)

Rhythm Etude No. 5
(F Major)

C Instruments
Alla marcia (♩ = 120-132)

B♭ Instruments
Alla marcia (♩ = 120-132)

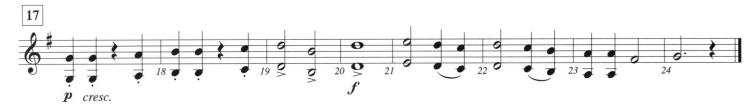

E♭ Instruments
Alla marcia (♩ = 120-132)

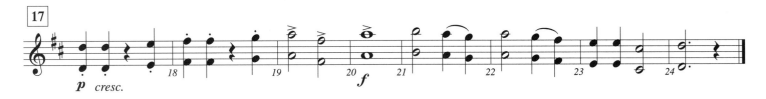

Rhythm Etude No. 5

(F Major)

F Instruments

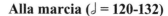

Bass Clef Instruments

Rhythm Etude No. 6
(D minor – ABA form)

Conductor's Score

Andante espressivo (♩ = 60-72)

Rhythm Etude No. 6
(D minor – ABA form)

C Instruments

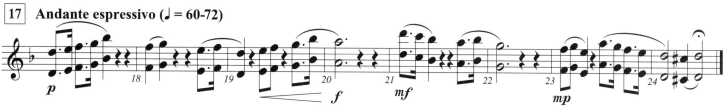

Bb Instruments

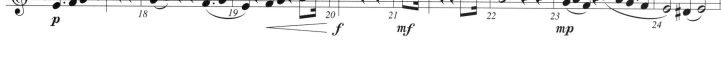

Eb Instruments

Rhythm Etude No. 6
(D minor – ABA form)

Rhythm Etude No. 7
(A♭ Major)

Conductor's Score
Moderato (♩ = 100-120)

Rhythm Etude No. 7
(A♭ Major)

Conductor's Score cont.

C Instruments

Rhythm Etude No. 7
(A♭ Major)

Rhythm Etude No. 7

(A♭ Major)

F Instruments

Bass Clef Instruments

BB206

Rhythm Etude No. 8

(F minor)

Conductor's Score

Allegro (♩ = 132-152)

Rhythm Etude No. 8
(F minor)

C Instruments

B♭ Instruments

E♭ Instruments

Rhythm Etude No. 8
(F minor)

F Instruments

Bass Clef Instruments

Rhythm Etude No. 9

(Db Major)

Conductor's Score

Allegro (♩ = 144-160)

Rhythm Etude No. 9
(D♭ Major)

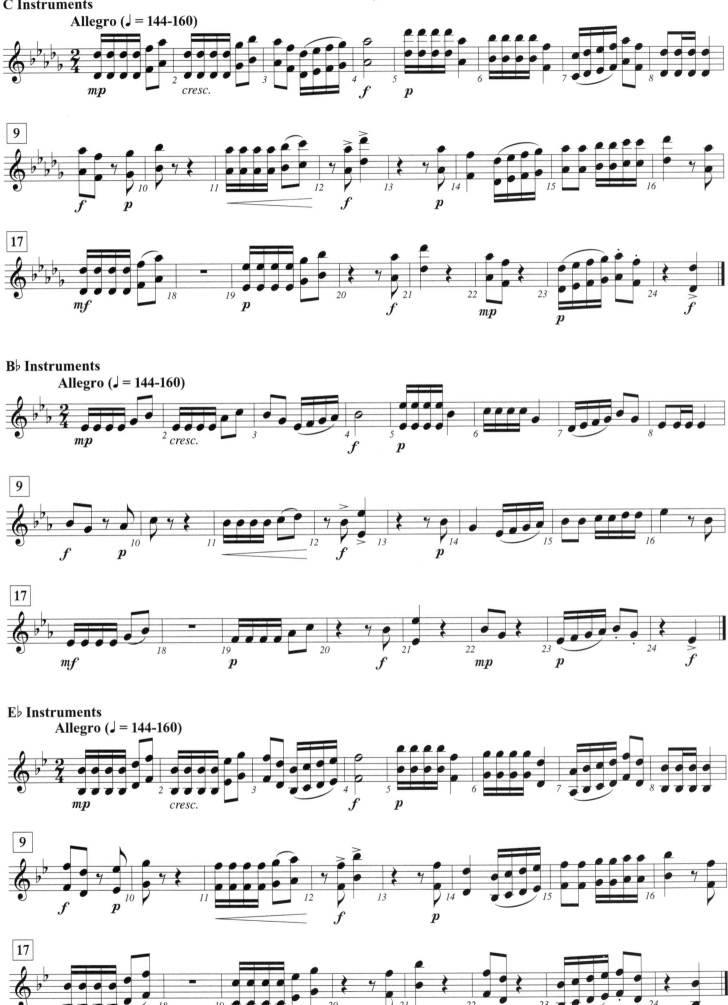

Rhythm Etude No. 9

(D♭ Major)

F Instruments

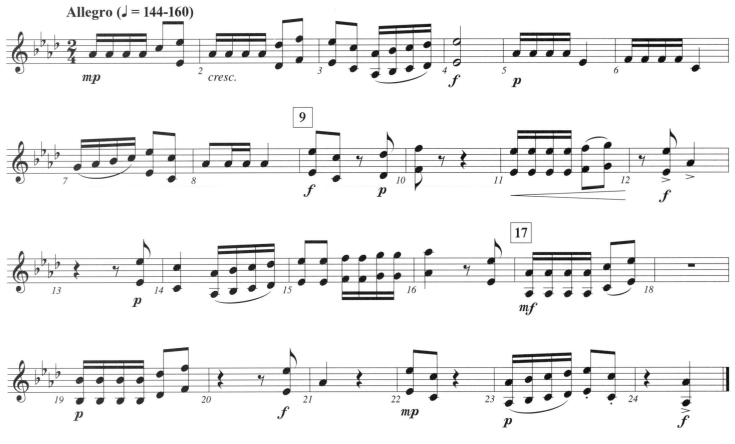

Bass Clef Instruments

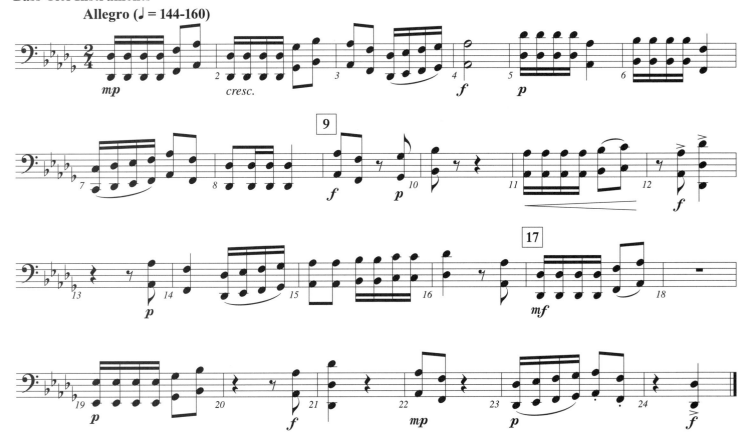

Rhythm Etude No. 10
(B♭ minor)

Conductor's Score

Rhythm Etude No. 10
(B♭ minor)

Conductor's Score cont.

C Instruments

Rhythm Etude No. 10
(B♭ minor)

Rhythm Etude No. 10
(B♭ minor)

F Instruments

Bass Clef Instruments

Rhythm Etude No. 11

(C Major – Pentatonic)

Conductor's Score

Rhythm Etude No. 11

(C Major – Pentatonic)

C Instruments

B♭ Instruments

E♭ Instruments

Rhythm Etude No. 11

(C Major – Pentatonic)

F Instruments

Bass Clef Instruments

Rhythm Etude No. 12

(A minor)

*𝄽. = 𝄾𝄿

Rhythm Etude No. 12

(A minor)

C Instruments

B♭ Instruments

E♭ Instruments

*𝄽· = 𝄾𝄾

BB206

Rhythm Etude No. 12
(A minor)

F Instruments

Andante (♩. = 80)

Bass Clef Instruments

Andante (♩. = 80)

*𝄽· = 𝄽 ♪

Rhythm Etude No. 13
(G Major)

Rhythm Etude No. 13
(G Major)

C Instruments

Allegro (♩. = 108-132)

B♭ Instruments

Allegro (♩. = 108-132)

E♭ Instruments

Allegro (♩. = 108-132)

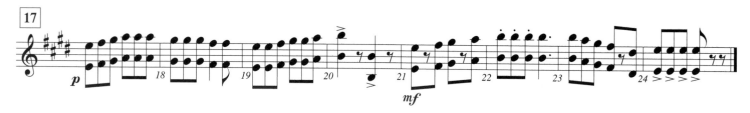

Rhythm Etude No. 13

(G Major)

F Instruments

Allegro (♩. = 108-132)

Bass Clef Instruments

Allegro (♩. = 108-132)

Rhythm Etude No. 14

(E minor)

Conductor's Score

Rhythm Etude No. 14

(E minor)

C Instruments

Allegretto (♩. = 100-120)

Rhythm Etude No. 14

(E minor)

B♭ Instruments

Rhythm Etude No. 14

(E minor)

F Instruments

Bass Clef Instruments

Rhythm Etude No. 15
(D Major)

Rhythm Etude No. 15
(D Major)

C Instruments
Moderato (♩ = 80-96)

Rhythm Etude No. 15
(D Major)

Bb Instruments

Eb Instruments

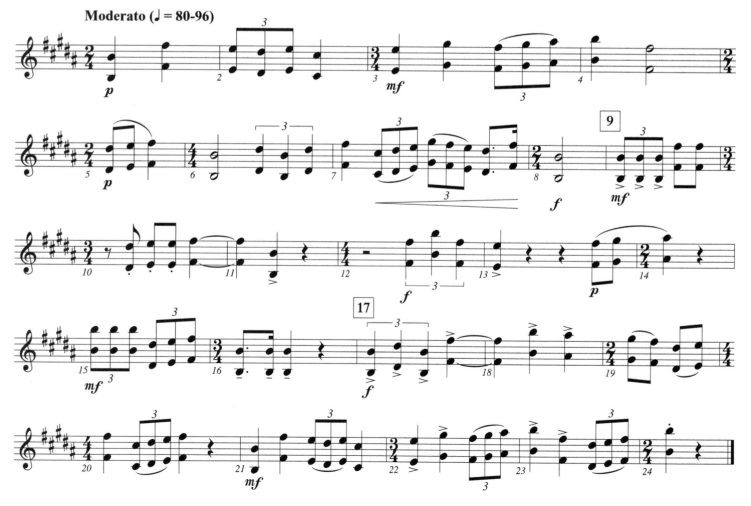

Rhythm Etude No. 15

(D Major)

F Instruments

Bass Clef Instruments

Rhythm Etude No. 16

(B minor)

Conductor's Score

Rhythm Etude No. 16
(B minor)

C Instruments

Allegro (♩. = 132–160)

Rhythm Etude No. 16
(B minor)

Bb Instruments

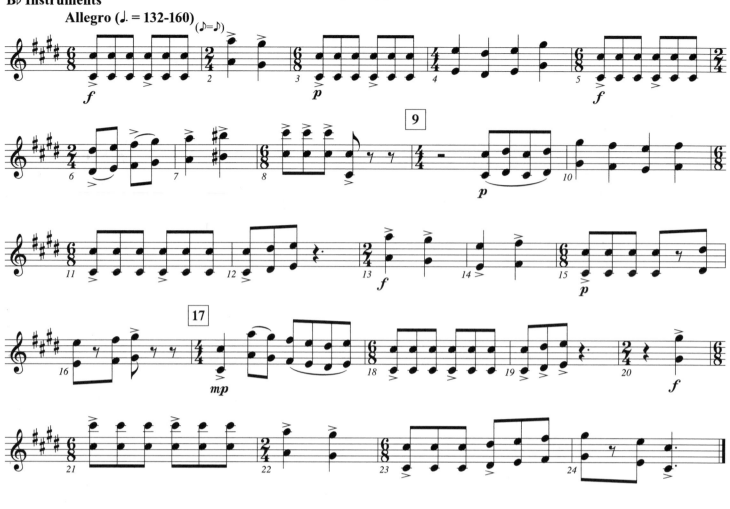

Eb Instruments

Rhythm Etude No. 16
(B minor)

F Instruments

Bass Clef Instruments

SUPERIOR BANDS IN SIXTEEN WEEKS

Quincy C. Hilliard
Text written and edited by
Deborah A. Sheldon

A Systematic Approach to Developing Superior
TONE, INTONATION, BALANCE, & TECHNIQUE
Ideal for Festival Preparation

BB204

One Book

provides systematic approaches to the following issues:

TONE

- Chorales for work on balance
- Chromatic warm-ups and lip-flexibility exercises

INTONATION

- Includes intonation tests, pitch tendencies, and suggestions for improving pitch specific to each individual instrument

BALANCE

- Balance Pyramid for proper blending and balance
- Warm-ups and tuning chorales

TECHNIQUE

- Scales in seconds and thirds, arpeggios, and chromatic scales
- Breath control exercises

INTEGRATED PERCUSSION RUDIMENTS

- Unlike any other book of its kind, this system incorporates progressive percussion rudiments throughout

FESTIVAL PREPARATION

- Notes to the director and student based on years of experience